THE ADVENTURES OF
BUCK FELNER

More great humor by John McPherson

Close to Home
High School Isn't Pretty
Life at McPherson High
McPherson Goes to Church
McPherson Goes to Work
McPherson's Marriage Album
McPherson on Parenting
McPherson's Sports and Fitness Manual

THE ADVENTURES OF BUCK FELNER

AS SEEN IN FOCUS ON THE FAMILY'S
BREAKAWAY MAGAZINE

JOHN McPHERSON

AUTHOR OF *LIFE AT McPHERSON HIGH*

ZondervanPublishingHouse

Grand Rapids, Michigan

A Division of HarperCollinsPublishers

The Adventures of Buck Felner
Copyright © 1995 by John McPherson

Requests for information should be addressed to:
Zondervan Publishing House
Grand Rapids, Michigan 49530

Library of Congress Cataloging-in-Publication Data

McPherson, John, 1959–
    The adventures of Buck Felner / John McPherson.
         p.   cm.
    Summary: A high school freshman describes such experiences as gym class, a first date, extracurricular activities, and Christmas vacation.
    ISBN: 0-310-48681-5 (softcover)
    [1. High schools—Fiction. 2. Schools—Fiction. 3. Humorous stories.]   I. Title.
PZ7.M478823Ad 1995
[Fic]-dc20   94-43860
                                                                                                      CIP
                                                                                                      AC

Interior design by Sue Koppenol

Printed in the United States of America

95 96 97 98 99 00 /❖DH/ 10 9 8 7 6 5 4 3 2 1

*To Greg Johnson
for his tremendous
support and friendship*

CONTENTS

It's Baaack! 9

Encounters with a Terminator 13

The Boredom Queen of Wimpler High 17

Some Serious Advice on Dating 21

The Invisible Man 27

The Thrill of the Hunt 31

How to Make the Most of Your Christmas Vacation 35

Getting Teed Off 41

Totally Cool 45

Hitting the Slopes 49

On a Roll 53

Testing One, Two, Three! 57

The Dating Game 61

Bulking Up 67

Attack of the Bloodmobile 71

Home Alone 75

Broadway Buck 79

Countdown to Summer 83

Working for a Living 87

Buck on Friends 91

Wheezin' Down the Highway 95

There's No Place Like Home 101

Water, Water Everywhere 105

IT'S BAAACK!

Whoever it was that put the calendar together and said that summer is officially over on September 21st was totally out to lunch. Sure, there are still leaves on the trees and, yeah, you've still gotta mow the lawn. But, hey, let's face it. Once you get inside that hideous yellow monster (I'm talking about a school bus), your summer is history, and pretty much all the fun has been vaporized from your life. SCHOOL IS BACK!

Okay, so we all agree. School is a drag, and most of us would rather dig trenches with a spoon than spend nine and a half months of every year trying to figure out what an imaginary number is and why we should care. But what exactly is it about school that makes dropping out and becoming a toll booth operator seem like such a tempting idea? Well, everybody's different, but there are just a few things about school that seriously detract from my enjoyment of life. Here they are, in no particular order.

1. Getting Up Early

I have a serious problem with getting up while most birds are still zonked out. This is due mostly to the fact that, although my body may be up and moving around and occasionally mumbling things, my brain does not wake up until sometime around 10:30. The net result is me doing things like brushing my teeth

with my socks, blow-drying my tongue, and wearing my mom's bedroom slippers to first period gym class. It doesn't help matters that my alarm clock sounds like something being electrocuted. Personally, I think it would make a lot more sense if school started around noon.

2. Comparing Tans

When you look around the halls on the first day of school here at Wimpler High, you'll see approximately two-thirds of the kids holding their forearms up to each other, arguing over whose looks more like a piece of beef jerky. In fact, many kids in our school consider tanning to be a major

athletic event, with rumors floating around that it's going to be made into a varsity sport. Several girls (I'm not gonna name any names here) have gone so far as to install tanning booths in their lockers. I, on the other hand, couldn't get a tan if I spent a week playing volleyball in the sun. Oh, sure, I can get sunburned in no time. Light sources such as flashlight beams and night lights have been known to give me second-degree burns in less than thirty seconds. And if I want to go to the beach, I'd better be sure to slap on at least three coats of oil-based house paint, or I'll come back looking like a mascot for Red Lobster.

So I pretty much avoid the sun and arrive at school strongly resembling the Pillsbury Doughboy. Comparing tans is one ritual I could do without.

3. Schedules

These things drive me nuts. You need to be either a decoding expert for the CIA or a specialist in Roman hieroglyphics just to figure out what and where your first class is. Here's part of my schedule for this year:

STDNT–FLNR, BCK 301–95–4211
PRD CLS TM LCT—TCHR
01 MSHP–102 0800–0855 PR–27 RSBBRN
02 BLGY-LB 0900–1015 CRP–17 FGMNZ
03 ALBG–107 1020–1125 CRNZ–14 LTRY
04 GLB–202 1130–1300 FRX–P1 NRKR

For all I know, this could be the launching instructions for a nuclear missile sight. My only hope is to wander the halls aimlessly waiting to hear my name during roll call. Last year I wrote two term papers and took a midterm in cultural geography before I figured out I was actually supposed to be in wood shop.

Now don't get me wrong. School does have its good points: food fights, dissecting things, burping contests in the cafeteria. And, when it gets right down to it, learning stuff is a pretty cool thing to do. After all, if it wasn't for school I'd probably still be finger-painting and trying to impress girls with my trike. No doubt about it. Dropping out of school would be a seriously boneheaded move. But I still keep hoping that one of these years the school officials are gonna goof up and make the school year two-and-a-half months long and summer nine-and-a-half months. I could get into that.

ENCOUNTERS WITH A TERMINATOR

Wayne Zartnik. Simply reading the name makes my stomach contract to the size of a walnut and my eyes roll back into my head so that I'm peering into my brain. When I actually hear his name my nose instantly starts to bleed, a stimulus response caused by the ever-looming fear that sometime very soon Wayne's fist will make repeated, sledgehammer-like contact with my face.

Fortunately, over the last nine years I have miraculously avoided being mutilated by Wayne. (Once by hiding in a drainage pipe for five hours and another time by making myself throw up to convince him that I had a highly contagious killer disease.)

You guessed it. Wayne is Wimpler High's designated bully. But calling Wayne a bully is like calling the Grand Canyon a ditch. Wayne's more like a terminator. I have seen Wayne beat guys to a pulp using only his forehead, usually for such minor infractions as his not liking the way they combed their hair. Wayne's image is not softened by the fact that he started shaving in third grade, has biceps the size of my waist, has more tattoos than the entire Navy, and should have graduated when Reagan was President.

As I said, reading Wayne's name normally gave me some pretty negative side effects. Under the circumstances, however, reading his name made me hyperventilate, lose control of all major muscle groups, and experience temporary blindness. According to the horrible piece of paper I held in my hand, Wayne Zartnik was my new locker mate.

Doomed to an entire year of close contact with someone who was rumored to eat live mice as snacks, I clamored for a way to save myself from certain annihilation. The only solution was obvious. I asked my dad if we could move to Australia. When he said no, I saw my life flash before my eyes, ending with a giant Zartnikian fist hurtling towards my face at warp speed.

Word of my fate spread quickly through school, and hundreds of people, even the principal, offered their condolences and said things like "It's been nice knowing you" or "I'll never forget you, Buck." Shirley Cosgrove asked if she could have my stereo.

I did my best to avoid locker 1302. For the first eleven days of school I wore my coat and carried all my books in a shopping bag. Things like my lunch and an extra pair of shoes I tied to my belt. I tried not to even walk past the locker, and when I did I walked rubbing up against the opposite wall, as though a huge, hairy, tattooed arm was going to leap from the locker and drag me screaming inside. Basically, I looked like a complete dork, but nobody said anything because they felt sorry for me.

But by the twelfth day of lugging around eighty pounds of books my arms were pretty close to being torn out of their sockets.

I was tired and humiliated and sick of being terrified of a locker. I wanted to just get punched out by Wayne and have it over with. Besides, with any luck Wayne was in prison somewhere and I was worrying about nothing.

I took a deep breath and walked toward the locker, sweating so badly that I left a slug-like trail down the hall. I slowly opened the locker, expecting Freddie Krueger to leap from its

innards. Instead I was hit on the head by a carton of cigarettes. The locker smelled like a horse stall magnified one hundred times and looked like a mini landfill. There was a leather jacket, some heavy metal posters, three or four knives (very comforting!), a large ball of hair (I didn't even want to guess where it came from!), and there was A LARGE HAND ON MY SHOULDER! It was him. Zartnik. The Beast. My nose started bleeding and I began stammering, "Uhh ... hello Mr. Zartnik, your honor, sir ..." but he cut me off, smiled, and said, "Hi! I'm Wayne Zartnik! You must be Buck. I was starting to wonder where you were. Hey, you need some Kleenex there! Sorry about the stench in the locker. You know how biology projects are. Oh, man! You must think I'm an ax murderer with those knives in there! I'm just sharpening them in metal shop for my dad."

I was speechless. This was not the Wayne Zartnik that I had heard about. He was speaking actual intelligent sentences, not grunting caveman-like syllables. He took biology. I couldn't see a single tattoo, and he had yet to punch me in the face. Basically, he was, well, nice.

Over the past few weeks Wayne and I have become pretty good friends. I'm not going to sugarcoat this and tell you that Wayne is a model citizen. He's got his share of problems. He smokes and probably drinks and definitely hangs with a pretty rough crowd. But underneath it all, he's a good guy. This whole thing has taught me a lot about rumors, and fears, and perceptions, and, to use a corny phrase, judging books by their covers. Mostly, I learned a lot about my own imagination.

There's one thing that still bothers me, though. I still can't figure out what that ball of hair in our locker is all about.

THE BOREDOM QUEEN OF WIMPLER HIGH

If you gave me a choice between sitting through a typical fifth period English class, taught by Mrs. Fendlestone, The Boredom Queen of Wimpler High, or eating a bowl of live crickets, I would eagerly wolf down the crickets. I'm starting to think she's got a second job as a hypnotist, because every time I'm in her class I feel like I drift into some kind of trance. I end up staring like a zombie at the back of the kid-in-front-of-me's neck for twenty or thirty minutes straight, trying to find interesting shapes among any moles he or she's got. I call them mole constellations.

No doubt I'm on my way to becoming a famous astronomer. One time I discovered this great mole constellation on the back of Alan Lupkowski's neck that looked just like Oprah Winfrey. I'm not kidding! She was holding a microphone and everything. I just about choked trying to keep from laughing. Man, was I ever tempted to whip out a felt-tipped pen and play connect-the-dots to make Oprah really stand out. But I wasn't exactly in the mood to get punched out in the middle of English class. (Lupko is an All-State linebacker.) Although it probably would have been a pleasant change from the excruciating boredom.

Last Wednesday, Fendlestone's class was even more boring than usual. You'd think that from the contorted looks on our

faces she could tell that we were all in a state of extreme mental pain from her droning. But she just kept going on and on about dangling participles. (Which, by the way, sound more like some sort of medical problem than a part of speech.)

I was killing time by staring at Dave Vargo's neck, trying to find a good mole constellation. Unfortunately, he had only two small moles, which meant the only constellations I could come up with were a javelin or pencil. Pretty dull stuff compared to Oprah Winfrey.

I started looking around the room to see what else was going on. Kyle Rimcard had fallen asleep on his desk. He looked like a total dufus when he awoke: indentations from a spiral notebook ran across his face, and an eraser was stuck to his forehead. I think just about everyone else was looking for mole constellations also. Except for Zack Westerman.

When I saw what Zack was doing, I think I sprained my sinuses trying not to laugh. Zack was catching flies in midair, shaking them around in his hands, and then throwing them down onto his desk. This left the flies stunned but basically unhurt. Then he'd take one of Shirley Cosgrove's hairs (she was sitting in front of him) and carefully tie it around the fly. After a couple of minutes the shaken insect would wake up and fly off, only to find itself tethered to Shirley's head.

When I first looked over, Zack had tied three flies to her head. But as time passed he kept adding more and more flies. She kept trying to wave them off, not knowing they were actually anchored to her head. By the time class had ended, Zack had lassoed eighteen flies, and Shirley looked like some kind of alien from a Star Trek episode: "The Humanoid No-Pest-Strip from Plant Zurp." It was a riot!

Fortunately for Zack, Shirley's got a pretty good sense of humor, so she didn't get too bent out of shape over it. Although Zack did discover a dead tuna in his book bag the next day—during the middle of third-period algebra.

These days, things are still boring as usual in English class. I did find a constellation on Donna Melby's neck that looks a lot like my brother being pecked in the head by a penguin. But nothing that tops Oprah.

Some Serious Advice on Dating

What's that, you say? After staking out every move Laura Hinquist has made for the past seventeen months (including following her around the mall disguised as a rhododendron), you finally got up the nerve to ask her out? And she said yes?! So you're going out tomorrow night and you've suddenly come down with a mongo case of the jitters ... because you don't have the slightest idea where to take her, or what to do, or what to say?!

Neither do I! But I do know what you *shouldn't* do or say.

How did I, a mere mortal guy, get my hands on these incredibly valuable centuries-old dating secrets which are not available in any stores? Simple! My best friend happens to be an actual certified girl who has experienced thousands of bone-headed maneuvers on the part of guys she's gone out with.

So when faced with the task of taking Lisa Fernmeld to the Spurkle County Taco Festival, I turned to Shirley for some expert advice. I said, "Shirley, what are some of the many stupid things that I should not do while on a date?" Here are the five things that Shirley said were at the top of her list of things guys shouldn't do on a date. She even suggests that I carry a copy of the list with me at all times for easy reference.

1. Don't talk with your mouth full.

Yeah, I know, this sounds like something your mom would say. But Shirley was out with this guy once who was talking and wolfing down a piece of pizza at the same time. When she got home that night, she discovered a hunk of pepperoni stuck to her forehead. My advice is to talk only when your mouth is *half* full (or less).

2. Don't take them to Wrestlemania.

According to Shirley, girls aren't into watching sweaty, three-hundred-pound guys with names like "Thor, the Regurgitator" give each other body slams while wearing bikini shorts that are too small for a third-grader. Don't ask me why they don't like it ... they're just weird that way.

3. Don't cut your fingernails in public.

This is a definite no-no. Shirley once went to Denny's with a guy who made a game out of trying to get his fingernail clippings to land on the plate behind them. She walked out after he accidentally landed one on her meatloaf.

4. Don't burp audibly.

Personally, I was pretty proud of myself when I was able to simultaneously burp and say "Good evening" the night I picked up Sue Wizkowski. But she and her mom didn't seem too impressed. Even though a lot of guys consider burping to be a

WHAT'S THE WORST
THAT COULD HAPPEN?
SHE TELLS ME SHE'S
NOT QUITE READY FOR
THAT YET AND I
SAY "FINE."

popular hobby, Shirley insists that most girls aren't into it. Bummer.

5. Don't drive with the windows down.

Girls have this hang-up about their hair. Studies have shown that a typical girl spends an average of four days getting her hair ready for a date. Shirley usually spends six or seven days before a date doing major surgery on her hair, and a few of her friends won't even talk on the phone unless their hair is done. Some girls even believe that having two hairs crossed is bad for the circulation in their brains! (Most guys, on the other hand, have no problem walking around in public looking like they just combed their hair with an electric drill.)

So, when faced with having to ride in a car with the windows down and subjecting her hair to any measurable amount of wind, don't be surprised if your date asks if she can ride in the trunk. (Really, it'll have nothing to do with being seen with you.)

So there you have it. Five things guys should never do while out on a date. According to Shirley, if you do even one of the things on the list, your chances of getting a second date drop to about one in three. Do *two* things, and your date will probably dial 911. Commit *three* of 'em, and girls at your school will start to substitute your name for the word *dweeb* in everyday conversation. (In fact, the word *dweeb* comes from a guy named Brian Dweeb, who, on May 16, 1977, actually did *four* of the things on this list.)

Okay, fine. I'm man enough to admit that we guys can occasionally goof up and behave like Neanderthals once in a while. But girls can be equally squid-like when they're out on dates. I kindly pointed this out to Shirley and suggested that she might want to have my list of "things that girls do that bug guys the most" tattooed  on her arm. She was not amused. Here it is anyway. I hope this information will be put to good use.

1. Too Much Makeup

This is a pretty common turn-off. You ask a girl out, and when you pick her up she looks like an Avon lady exploded in her face. I took out this girl named Janice Wagler once who had on false eyelashes that looked like tentacles. I didn't kiss her goodnight because I was afraid her eyelashes would tangle themselves in mine and we'd have to go to the emergency room to get surgically detached. So I played it safe and just shook her hand. So much for playing it safe! I wound up getting stabbed in the palm by one of her four-inch long machete-like fingernails.

2. Overdressing

This turn-off is along the same lines as wearing too much makeup. My friend Marty had a good example for this one. He invited a girl to play mini-golf with him one night and she showed up in a fancy white dress, dangly earrings that looked like some sort of Christmas tree ornament, high heels that made

OR, SHE BODY-SLAMS ME SO HARD THAT THE PATTERNS ON THE RUG BECOME PERMANENTLY EMBEDDED IN MY SKIN.

her taller than most players in the NBA, and—this is what really got to him—gloves! She was wearing those skintight type of gloves that require an exacto-knife to get off. Meanwhile, Marty felt like a complete dufus because he was wearing jeans and a T-shirt that said "Bubba's Truckstop and Flea Market."

3. Obsession with Dieting

Few things can be more aggravating for a guy than to save up for weeks to take a girl out to dinner and have her order a small plate of celery stalks. We hate this mostly because it makes us look like crazed food mongers for eating something like T-bone steak. Shirley is a classic example of this dating flaw. Whenever we grab something to eat, she inevitably finishes off her celery stalks in about two minutes and spends the rest of the time staring at me as though I'm devouring Bambi for dinner, occasionally reciting irritating facts like "Did you know that a ten-ounce steak has more calories than fifty pounds of steamed radishes?" Whatever you say, Shirley.

One girl I dated was convinced that you could get excess calories by inhaling dust and pollen. As a result, she always wore one of those white dust masks, looking like she was about ready to start belt-sanding the living room floor. She also thought you could gain weight by licking stamps. One time she asked a postal clerk if they had any diet stamps.

So anyway, girls, feel free to pig out a bit on dates. You'll make us feel a lot better about ourselves.

4. Looking at Your Watch Every Five Minutes

Don't do this, please! It makes us paranoid! When we're out with a girl who is constantly looking at her watch, we immediately start thinking: *She's looking at her watch! What's wrong? She must want to go home! Maybe I need another carton of breath mints! Maybe she thinks I'm a dork! Maybe she's mad at me because I burped the entire "Back to the Future" theme song in the middle of the restaurant!*

You can see the damaging effects that looking at your watch can have on a guy's emotional well-being, so try to avoid it whenever possible.

5. Chewing Gum

This one can really grate on a guy's nerves, especially if you make that annoying snapping noise that a lot of gum chewers make. I remember cruising around in my car with a girl named Lois one time. I looked over at her and I thought the airbag on her side of the car had inflated. It turned out that she had blown this bubble about the size of Wyoming. She looked like one of those dorky clown things that they use to inflate balloons. She maintained the bubble for about five minutes and then it exploded, sending shock waves through the car. It took me about four weeks to get all the little flecks of gum off the right side of my head, and my ears rang for a couple of months.

Now that Shirley and I have outlined the things that guys and girls *shouldn't do* on dates, we really wish we could fill you in on what we all *should* do. Unfortunately, neither of us has a clue in that department.

The Invisible Man

It's time once again for basketball in gym class! Jammin' down the court, catching a quick bounce pass, and slammin' that baby home! I love it! There's only one problem. I can't *do* it! My version is more like spazzin' down the court, kicking a quick bounce pass, and slammin' into the wall. Yep, on the ecological chart of basketball skill levels, I rank behind amphibians, and just slightly above pond scum.

Gym class basketball starts with a twisted version of the NBA draft. You know the routine. The gym teacher appoints two jock-brained captains whose job it is to totally demoralize the rest of us by picking teams as though we were entrants in a cattle auction.

There are three kinds of gym class basketball draft picks: (1) guys who get picked first, (2) middle-of-the-pack guys, and (3) guys that most captains wouldn't pick unless the gym teacher threatened to floss their teeth with a dirty gym sock. Some qualities that will make you a prime candidate for number 3 status are: wearing red rubber snow boots to gym class, constantly wiping your nose on your arm, having your gym shorts on backwards, and having scored seven points for the other team during the last game.

Since being picked last in gym class ranks right up there with going to a prom with your Aunt Ethel in terms of social life disintegration, we draft pickees will do anything to better our

27

YEAH! THE BUCKSTER
SLAMS ANOTHER ONE!
INCREDIBLE HANG-TIME!

SWOOSH!

AMAZING! FELNER
STRIKES AGAIN!
HE'S UNSTOPPABLE!

THWANK!

chances. Some popular techniques include: combing your hair straight up to give the illusion that you are 6'6", getting a tattoo that says "Bubba" to make you look tougher, and whining, "Please pick me! I won't mess up this time! *Please!* Oooh! Oooh!"

Unfortunately, none of these techniques ever works for me. In fact, one time a captain picked the home economics teacher over me (she just happened to be walking by on her way to the nurse to get a battery for her hearing aid). It's not that I'm completely useless at basketball. I can dribble *great*. I just can't dribble and run at the same time. (I can't even *breathe* and dribble at the same time.) If they would just create a new position, the designated dribbler, I'd probably be playing varsity. "Now dribbling for Wimpler High, *Buck Felner*!" I'd go out, dribble in place for a minute or so (holding my breath, of course), pass the ball to an actual player, and people would cheer. That would be cool.

Instead, I am reduced to goober-basketball status, which is pretty much like being the invisible man. I could be wide open, next to the basket, standing on a step ladder, and the pass would go to some guy who's got more guys guarding him than the President. I don't really even *want* the ball. I'd settle for the honor of being guarded! Occasionally I do make a deal with the other invisible man, the kid on the other team who got picked next to last, whereby we agree to guard each other. This helps

AMAZING! FELNER STRIKES AGAIN! HE'S UNSTOPPABLE!

THWANK!

RATS!

keep us both from getting lonely and gives anybody watching the impression that we are actually playing. It gets to be like a game of one-on-one. He'll cruise down to one end, and I'll guard him like crazy. Then we'll turn around and he'll guard me. The only weird thing about our game of one-on-one is that we don't have a ball.

Believe it or not, however, somebody did pass me the ball once. It happened last year. As usual, I was about three hundred yards from the nearest other player, when this new kid, not realizing that I was a well-known basketball-dufus, passed me the ball! The whole gym fell silent, stunned by this outrageous move. Everyone could tell by the look in my eyes that I meant business. Years of being picked last had culminated in this one great golden opportunity. I dribbled steadily, coolly, with a shrewd, knowing look on my face, a man with a mission. And then, without warning, I made my move. I fired a red-hot bullet pass, and everybody watched in awe as the ball screamed through the air ... and smacked the janitor right in the side of his head, knocking him onto the floor and spilling his scrub bucket onto the court. I had seen him out of the corner of my eye and, for some dorko reason, thought he was a wide open teammate. In short, I completely spazzed out.

This year I'm sure I'll be back to playing one-on-one with my fellow invisible man. I'm pretty fired up though, because I've got some new moves that I know will leave me wide open.

The Thrill of the Hunt

You'd think that buying a Christmas tree would be a pretty simple process. You go out, find a tree, and ask yourself three basic tree-oriented questions: (a) Is it green? (b) Does it have any needles on it? and (c) Are there any rabid animals living in it that will lunge at our eyeballs right about the time we start putting on the tinsel? (Correct answers are (a) yes, (b) yes, and (c) no.) Unfortunately, this is not the way it works with our family. Whereas normal Christmas tree shopping should be about as involved as buying a pair of socks, my family picks out a Christmas tree more cautiously than most people would choose a brain surgeon.

Traditionally, The Great Felner Christmas Tree Hunt begins on the first Saturday of December. Every year my dad discovers a new and highly secret Christmas tree farm that is invariably thirty miles further away than last year's secret Christmas tree farm. (SCTF's, as Dad calls 'em.) This year I'm positive we'll drive through at least two time zones to get to the target SCTF.

In order to keep any of the neighbors from following us to the secret location, Dad insists that we leave at 3:00 A.M. and drive with the lights off for about the first ten miles. Two years

ago he started making us smear grease on our faces, "just to be on the safe side," he said. Mom was not psyched. When we finally do get there (usually sometime the next day) we discover that approximately seven million other dads also knew about the SCTF, and therefore the entire population of Michigan and much of Canada is already there, hungry for a primo Christmas tree. There's nothing like stomping through the woods with hordes of people carrying chain saws to get me in the holiday spirit.

But the mob scene doesn't dampen Dad's quest for the perfect tree. He approaches the whole thing as though we were out hunting grizzlies. "OK, everybody fan out. Buck, head north. Louis [my seven-year-old mutant brother], cut to the west [Louis doesn't have a clue which way is west]. Doris [code name for Mom], cover the eastern sector. I'll circle around to the south and try to cut 'em off. There are some good ones out there. I can smell 'em!"

Unfortunately, Dad's always a bit out of touch regarding the quality of the available trees. Thanks to the armies of saw-wielding tree-manglers that got there before us, the place looks like a nuclear test site. Tall weeds start to look like pretty tempting tannenbaums. Nonetheless, we keep tromping around, convinced that we'll find a tree suitable for display in The White House, or at least one that still has needles.

After about seven hours of aimless wandering, we start the formal tree selection process, not because we've seen any decent trees (we haven't), but because of three other very important factors: (1) it is –20° F out, with gusts near seventy miles per hour and windchill approaching absolute zero, (2) it got dark an hour ago, and (3) there are no bathrooms. By about 5:30 P.M. several of our major arteries have frozen solid, and it is so dark that we now have to judge the trees by touch, smell, and in Louis's case, taste (I told you he was a mutant). Eventually, one of us yells "Here's a nice one!" which immediately starts a stampede of five or six hundred non-Felners thinking that the person yelling was someone from their hunting party. This usually results in the chosen tree being trampled beyond recognition. On the rare occasions that the tree doesn't get annihilated, somebody in the family whines "It's not *full* enough!" and we all turn away like zombies and start feeling and sniffing more trees.

Fortunately, after about ten hours of agony, The Great Felner Christmas Tree Hunt comes to an end. It never ends because we found a great tree, or because we're so hungry we've started to eat pine cones, or because our nostrils have frozen shut. It ends because Louis has passed out due to sheer exhaustion, and the remaining three of us agree to go with whatever tree is closest to Louis's head. I like to think of it as Christmas tree roulette. Louis could save us all a lot of trouble if he'd just pass out about nine hours earlier.

How to Make the Most of Your Christmas Vacation

Well, you made it! You've just survived four days of nonstop midterms, with questions like "What's the cube root of 118,794.129?" (no calculators allowed), "What's the average caloric intake of the Himalayan Spit Beetle?" and "In 5,000 words or more, compare and contrast the following: Whitney Houston and the federal deficit." You've also heard *Frosty the Snowman* played over the school's PA system for the 4,973rd time, been approached by over a hundred mindless twits who say "See ya next year! Get it?! *Next* year?!" and had an entire can of that fake snow stuff sprayed on the back of your head by an upperclassman. You deserve a break. You deserve *Christmas* break.

Unfortunately, Christmas break is merely an oasis in that vast desert known as the school year. You've got fourteen, maybe fifteen days tops, and it is essential that you use them wisely. Here are some ways to insure yourself of a memorable Christmas vacation.

1. Make Your Own Christmas Gifts

Here are the hard facts. You've got about six days to do the same amount of Christmas shopping that your mom has been working on, virtually nonstop, since July. The only way you can possibly achieve this feat is to do a highly dangerous thing. You must go to a mall. And if you go to a mall in late December you will become either (a) lost, (b) trampled, or (c) trampled and then lost. Furthermore, most of you probably aren't even old enough to drive to a mall, and even if you were you wouldn't be able to get a parking spot until sometime around St. Patrick's Day.

So what's the solution to this dilemma? Very simple. Make your own Christmas gifts. With a little creativity and about three bucks (even *less* if you go through your neighbors' garbage) you can churn out dozens of exciting Christmas gifts using everyday items found lying around the house. Not only will you avoid getting lost or trampled, you'll also save some big bucks. Here are a few examples of the many gifts you could make for family members:

- Dad will be the talk of the office when he shows up in the dress pants you made for him entirely out of aluminum foil. Aluminum pants are shrink-proof *and* stain-proof. (Be sure to warn Dad *not* to wear the pants on hot sunny days or during electrical storms.)

- Never mind spending sixty dollars on that extravagant *Ode-Du-Yak* perfume that your sister wants. For about eight cents, you can turn a packet of cherry Kool-Aid into a great batch of perfume that Sis will love. Put it in a plastic milk jug, slap a label on it, and she'll never know the difference. (Except for the fact that she'll be licked by dogs and small children wherever she goes.)
- Why fork over $149.57 for that Inter-Galactic Neutron Space telescope that your little brother wants when you can make a near duplicate with a couple of paper towel rolls and some of your dad's old eyeglass lenses? Your brother will think he's the next Carl Sagan.
- And for Mom, you can easily weave a pair of great-looking nylon stockings out of fishing line and old dental floss.

2. Decorate the Dog

Sure, I know, this sounds stupid. But is it really any more bizarre than decorating a tree? With a string of lights and a bat-

tery pack old Duke will look like a canine version of the Macy's Christmas Parade. Furthermore, if you live on a busy street, you'll have the added satisfaction of knowing that your pooch will be easily spotted by oncoming cars (most of which will drive off the road in fits of hysteria because they'll think they're being chased by some kind of mutant Christmas tree).

3. Have Your Gifts Scanned

Dying to find out what's in your Christmas gifts? Forget about the unreliable shake-the-gifts method! Take your gifts to the airport, act like you're leaving on a flight, and as the gifts are being x-rayed by Security, look over their shoulders to see what's inside. Why agonize for days wondering if you're getting that solar powered boom-box?

4. Write Your History Paper Entirely on Styrofoam Packing Peanuts

Have you ever wondered what to do with the 4,786,271 styrofoam peanuts that inevitably engulf your house on Christmas Day (besides seeing how many you can convince your little brother to stick up his nose)? Think no more! No doubt you were assigned some kind of hideous term paper the day before vacation, such as, "Describe in 27,000 words the role of 'Happy Days' reruns in the break-up of the Soviet Union." Your teacher surely requested that it be typed, but did she say "typed on paper"? Probably not! So get even *plus* help the environment by doing it all on styrofoam peanuts. Type one word per peanut and keep them in order by making a garland out of them with a needle and thread. Or, forget about keeping them in order and just put them in a box and let her figure out what order they're supposed to be in. At the very least, she's got to give you an A for originality.

5. The Ten-Yard Needle Dash

If your living room is anything like mine the week after Christmas, it's covered with approximately eight jillion dried pine needles. This is due to the fact that everyone in our family assumes that someone else watered the tree. (Plus, on the rare occasion that someone *does* water the tree, the dog sucks it all up.) For a real challenge, get some of your friends together and see who can walk the furthest distance across the living room *barefoot* without screaming or passing out. The record in our household is seventeen feet, nine-and-a-half inches by my cousin Lenny, who is recovering nicely.

6. Take Down the Christmas Tree Ornaments Using Only Your Teeth

Without a doubt, one of the most dreaded tasks of the holiday season is de-trimming the Christmas tree. Here's a great way to turn a dull task into an exciting game. Try removing the tree ornaments using only your teeth! Score points as follows:

Decoration	Point Value
tinsel	1 point per strand
bulbs	2 points each
extremely delicate ornaments	3 points each
those ornaments that your mom likes to stick way in next to the trunk	5 points each

an entire string of lights
(without letting any
portion of the string
touch the ground)   10 points

any broken ornaments   –5 points

any accidentally swallowed
ornaments   –10 points

the star   20 points

the entire tree,
hauled out to the road   50 points

Remember, no stools or ladders allowed! For an added challenge try playing blindfolded!

So there you have it. Six great ways to make the most of your Christmas break. Now if we could only figure out a way to get two weeks off for Groundhog Day.

GETTING TEED OFF

As far as P.E. goes, January has never been a good month. Basketball ended in December, and volleyball doesn't start until February. So January ends up being sort of an athletic no-man's-land. All through Christmas vacation my gym teacher wracks his brain to devise new, more creative ways to push us to our athletic limits.

In the past we've been subjected to a wide variety of demented athletic challenges. Some of the more memorable ones are:

1. Chipmunk hockey (although now banned by our local Society for the Prevention of Cruelty to Animals, this game featured opposing teams trying to chase a live chipmunk into the other team's goal).
2. Dodge Jell-O (a twisted version of dodgeball using a large Jell-O cube instead of a ball).
3. Roller-tennis (pretty much the same as regular tennis, except you're wearing roller skates and smacking into walls a lot).

No January phys. ed. session would be complete without a healthy dose of the always dorky crab soccer. This is where players writhe around the floor on their hands and feet like total idiots, trying to kick a ball (roughly the size of a small planet) into the other team's goal. A better name for this sport would be survival, since players spend most of their time trying to avoid being

permanently embedded in the gym floor by the Pluto-sized ball. ("Hey! Isn't that Buck Felner over there by the foul line?!" "Yeah, didn't you hear? He got run over by a crab soccer ball and was instantly fossilized!")

So based upon previous January gym class experiences, we were pretty psyched about this year's brainstorm: golf. No half-crazed, rabid chipmunks involved. No getting slimed with Jell-O. No getting crushed by a crab soccer ball. Cool! Or so we thought.

Up until now, my golfing experience consisted of knocking an obnoxiously colored ball into the nostril of a giant clown at Manny's Mighty Mini-Golf. But I'd seen golf on TV, so

I felt like I'd pretty much mastered it. How hard could it be? A bunch of guys wearing clothes nice enough to wear to church walk up, hit the ball, and then collect prize checks large enough to purchase small island nations. I could get into that!

Our gym teacher, Mr. Clegman, lined us up with golf balls resting on fake grass mats. I thought for sure I'd be a natural. I had just one minor problem: I couldn't hit the ball! Not even once in 693 attempts! I don't think I could have hit a buffalo if it had been sitting on the ball. I felt like I was trying to hit a BB using a three-foot radio antenna.

Mr. Clegman, sensing that I was having fantasies of wrapping the golf club around the guy next to me, chimed in with some helpful tips. "Head down! Bend your knees! Arms straight! Stomach in! Swing your hips! Flare your nostrils! Curl your lips! Flex your pancreas!" And so on. After a while, I got confused and thought I was playing "Simon Says."

Day Two of our golfing disaster was a completely different story. All of us, including me, started to connect. In fact, we started to connect a little *too* well. As we watched rock-hard golf balls ricochet off the gym walls at one hundred miles per hour, it suddenly dawned on us that maybe, just maybe, driving golf balls in an enclosed space with thirty other people wasn't a tremendously bright idea. It was like being in the middle of some kind of sci-fi combat movie: "Attack of the PGA Tour."

Guys were dropping all around me. Above the screams, you could hear cries of "I'm hit!" "Medic!" and "I'm gonna make a break for the locker room! Cover me!"

Incredible feats of bravery were displayed as guys dragged fallen comrades to safety or took golf balls in the thigh to save a fellow classmate. In one astonishing act of heroism, two guys sneaked up behind a golf club, grabbed it in midswing, and wrestled it to the ground.

Mr. Clegman quickly called an end to the slaughter and asked for a casualty report: seventeen wounded, six missing in action (they were later found hiding in the shower), and four guys who couldn't remember their names. There were fifteen broken gym lights, eleven splintered bleacher seats, and a basketball rim that had been knocked completely off its backboard. Golf balls were found as far away as the biology lab, and there were even reports of some minor casualties in the faculty lounge.

Needless to say, there were no complaints when, on the next day of gym class, Mr. Clegman rolled out the crab soccer ball. Some guys even went up and kissed it. Sure, a few more guys got embedded in the gym floor, and a goalie did get knocked through a wall, but it was nothing compared to the fiasco that became known as "The Great Top-Flite Massacre."

TOTALLY COOL

I'm sitting here in the cafeteria with Shirley Cosgrove and Marty Fishman. Shirley and I are watching Marty suck milk through a straw into his nose. He's per-fected this talent to the point where he can suck it up into his left nostril while simultaneously sending it out of his right. Gross, but entertaining.

Meanwhile, Shirley is wearing a pair of earrings that her brother made for her in metal shop. They look like some sort of fishing lures. As I look at my two best friends, one thought pops into my head: *Man, are we a bunch of dufuses, or what?!*

In stark contrast to us, and sitting a mere two tables away, are "the cool people." You know who I'm talking about. Every school's got 'em. They pretty much require that you get a fed-eral permit just so you can say hi to them in the hall. They never notice one of us unless our hair is on fire. And even then it's just to complain that we're get-ting soot on their $400 limited-edition Air Jordans.

Sure, I'd love to be able to hang out with them. Everybody would. Why? Because they're *cool*. But I stand a better chance of being drafted by the New York Knicks than becoming part of the cool crowd.

What I want to know is what makes *them* so cool. Do they go to coolness camp in the summer? I can't figure it out. But I think fashion has a lot to do with it. For instance, take the old acid-washed jeans trend. What was the deal with those things? Somebody's mom accidentally uses Drano to do the laundry, and suddenly you're a dork if you've got normal-looking jeans. For some reason, if you're cool, it's okay to dress like a complete zipwad. In fact, in many cases, the stupider a cool person dresses, the cooler they become. (A perfect example is Madonna, who looks like she got her wardrobe from the planet Zorpan.)

So I told Marty, "Hey, why don't *we* dress like total zipwads? We can start a fad where we wear flannel pajama bottoms instead of jeans. It'll catch on, and we'll be considered ULTRA-cool!" So we did—for an entire week, and were called *dork, nerd, dweeb, dufus* and *geek* 1,184 times. And that was just from the teachers.

While we were getting abused for flannel pajama bottoms, jocks walked around school in shirts that resembled fish nets (and smelled like fish nets) and had been cut off so they came down to about two inches below their armpits. These things don't even provide the normal function of clothes (such as warmth), and look like they got caught in a lawn mower. Yet these guys are treated like they're the cast of "Beverly Hills 90210." I really don't get it.

For as long as I can remember there have been two kinds of people: the cool people and everyone else (who would gladly gargle hot tar if it would make them cool). Then, right after spring break, along came this kid named Lance Twitchell, who wasn't cool and didn't care that he wasn't cool. Everybody thought it was really cool that Lance didn't want to be cool. So suddenly, Lance became cool. And all the cool people wanted to hang out with Lance because he was so cool. Lance kept saying, "Hey! Knock it off! I don't want to be cool!" And people thought *this* was even cooler, to the point where Lance became this sort of coolness king. Other people started going around saying, "Hey, I don't want to be cool." But it didn't work, because people knew that they were only saying they didn't want to be cool so that they could become cool.

So what's the moral here on being cool? The best way to become cool is to stop worrying about whether or not you're actually cool. Hey, that's *really* cool with me. Now I can go ahead and try to break my personal record of stacking twenty-two Jell-O cubes on my forehead. Who cares if it's not cool?

Hitting the Slopes

I was extremely fired up when I heard what our upcoming church youth group outing was—a night of skiing, including transportation, rental equipment, lift passes, lessons, and hospitalization. I could see myself strutting around in outrageous looking $2,000 ski duds, flying down the slopes so fast that if I stuck out my arms I'd become airborne, and then hanging out by the lodge's fireplace surrounded by twenty or thirty girls who firmly believed that I was captain of the U.S. Ski Team. Unfortunately, things like this never go quite the way I expect them to. My big ski adventure was no exception.

The first clue that things were not going to be perfect was the bus that picked us up. It was made of wood and had no seats. I think it was an old hay wagon that had been converted into a bus by an over-ambitious shop class. About forty-seven other innocent victims and I were herded onto the bus and hauled off to the slopes. Three kids who had gone on the same youth group outing last year started to whimper. We all began to wonder what lay ahead.

The next step in our alpine adventure was getting our rental equipment. Rental equipment, we learned, is just like regular ski equipment except that it's got some kind of minor flaw, such as the bindings having been installed on the bottom of

the skis. A guy named Brad pawed through what appeared to be the wreckage of an airliner crash and started passing out our skis, poles, and boots. I got one ski that was about two feet longer than the other ski, but I didn't complain. The kid next to me was given a water ski.

We all started putting on our boots and discovered that, for some unknown reason, ski boots weigh just slightly less than Skylab. Once you've got them on, doing something basic, like turning around to wave to a friend, takes about forty-five minutes. If you've got to do something more involved, such as go

to the bathroom, you need to start moving two or three days in advance. Fortunately for us, our youth pastor hauled us out to the slopes one by one on those metal dollies they use to move vending machines around. As for the comfort level of ski boots, you can get a pretty good idea of how they feel by going out into the driveway and dropping a bowling ball on your foot fifty or a hundred times and then slamming it in the car door for good measure.

Now that we were out on the slopes we were at last ready to experience the thrill of seriously injuring ourselves. Our instructor, Ron, decided it was best to start us out on the Bunny Slope (which is ski lingo for "where the dorks ski"). I'm sure that to you hot-doggers out there skiing the Bunny Slope is about as thrilling as skiing across your living room. But to us it was like we were staring into the Grand Canyon. The slope was strewn with several hundred other beginners, most of whom were either lying face down in the snow or were lodged in trees. There were a few others who were crawling back up the hill, hoping to escape their instructors and make a break for the bus.

As we stared at the carnage below, Ron briefed us on the ever-popular "snow-plow" technique, whereby you twist your skis in towards each other far enough that you dislocate your knees while simultaneously crouching down so low that the tips of your skis go well up into your nose. When done properly, doing a snow-plow achieves the same effect as screaming at the top of your lungs, "I AM A COMPLETE GOOBER!!!"

The main reason that ski instructors teach the snow-plow technique is so you will be able to ski slowly and possibly survive long enough to return and buy their ridiculously expensive lift tickets another time. I, however, developed my own technique for slowing down whereby I skied directly into a tree at fifty miles per hour. When there weren't any trees around I used other skiers to bring me to a stop, although I definitely preferred trees, since they didn't scream.

I won't horrify you with the rest of the gory details of my alpine disaster. All I can say is I wasn't sorry when it was over. I knocked over more people in one night of skiing than most NFL linebackers do in a lifetime, had a pine cone go so far up my nose it had to be removed with needle-nosed pliers, and got frostbite on several portions of my brain. When it comes time to choose next winter's youth group outing I'll be lobbying heavily for a snowman building contest.

On a Roll

So there I was. Friday night at Rollermania, and things were not going well. I was wearing a pair of rental skates that no doubt had previously been worn by half the population of the United States. They stunk like road kill, and I had thirty or forty flies swarming around me to prove it. To top it off, one of the wheels on my right skate was stuck, so I wound up skating in circles about three feet in diameter. And over the rink's speaker system came an announcement that made me want to scream in fear: "OUR NEXT SONG IS COUPLES' SKATE ONLY!"

Now, if you're a girl, "couples' skate only" is no big deal. You can sit back and if you get asked to skate, fine. If not, you get to hang out and down three or four bags of Cheese Wads. But if you're a guy, you've got two options, either of which can reduce your social life to mildew.

The first is to also hang out on the sidelines and eat Cheese Wads. But if you do this, you might as well get a tattoo on your forehead that says "Loser." The girls eating Cheese Wads will

think you're a jerk for not asking them to skate, and every *guy* who *is* skating will think you're a wimp.

PACKED WITH 300 OTHER GUYS WHO ALREADY THOUGHT OF IT!

Your second option is to do the unthinkable. You must ask an actual, live, breathing girl to skate with you. Personally, I would rather walk up to the entire football team and tease them about their 0–and–10 season.

What was I so afraid of? I was afraid that if I asked a girl to skate, the music would suddenly stop and the rink would become deadly silent. Everyone would stare at us as if this were the gunfight at the OK Corral. And in a voice that measured seven on the Richter scale, she'd say: "*Me*?! Skate with *you*?! *Buck Felner*?! You've *got* to be kidding! AH HA! HA HA! HA HA!"

At this point the entire skating rink would erupt into laughter loud enough to attract several local news teams—who would make me the feature story on the eleven o'clock news: "Tonight's top story: Felner kid makes complete idiot of himself at local skating rink."

Hanging out on the sidelines sucking down several tons of Cheese Wads began to look pretty appealing. But I couldn't stomach the thought of wimping out this time. Besides, Cheese Wads give me a skin rash that makes me look like the victim of some kind of horrible chemical accident.

My best chance, I reasoned, was to establish eye contact with a girl. Unfortunately, eye contact was not my gift. The only living being I can remember making any kind of eye contact with was our neighbor's dog, who responded by biting me on the forehead. Add this to the fact that these girls were cruising by at fifty or sixty miles an hour and I was wearing skates that smelled like a dead woodchuck, and my chances for making meaningful eye contact dropped to slightly less than the chances of winning the State Lottery. But … I gave it a shot.

Girls skated toward me and I did what I could to make eye contact, mostly by wiggling my eyebrows, staring like a crazed zombie, and occasionally crossing my eyes. The only response I got was from a woman in her sixties who asked me if I needed a doctor. I probably did, but I thanked her and said no.

And then a weird thing happened. I suddenly started skating toward this one girl. It was as though my body was rebelling against my wimpy brain. I skated right up to her and asked her to skate. She said, "I can't. I have to floss my teeth."

It was just about the lamest excuse I'd ever heard. But, hey, it didn't matter! I'd proved to myself I wasn't a loser! I was able to hang out on the sidelines and hold my head high knowing that, unlike the guys standing around me, I at least had the guts to *try* asking a girl to skate.

It was a glorious moment in my young life. And it lasted for almost twenty minutes. Until I heard again those words that made me want to give up skating for good: "It's that time again. Couples' skate only!"

Testing One, Two, Three!

Now that we've scratched and clawed our way through two-thirds of another school year, I thought I should take the time to talk about a very painful subject. Tests.

If you're anything like me, your pulse has just jumped to about four thousand beats per minute, you're sweating like a sumo wrestler after the Japanese National Championships, and your stomach has just clenched shut and is starting to crawl slowly up into your mouth, all from merely reading the word *test*. (I experience dizziness and sudden hair loss just from seeing one of those emergency broadcast test patterns on TV!) I guess you could say I suffer from extreme examaphobia, which in plain English means that I would rather jump into a vat of live rats while wearing a suit made out of cheese than take a test.

Unfortunately, no teacher has offered the rats as an option, so I'm forced to deal with tests the same way everybody else does. Namely, I study until my eyeballs swell to twice their normal size while secretly hoping that the school will get sucked into a black hole the night before the test.

Probably the best way for me to conquer my fear of tests is to talk about them. Here are my thoughts on some of the more excruciating types of tests.

Pop Quizzes

If you ask me, these things should be outlawed by the Geneva Convention. One minute you're staring serenely at the kid next to you, fascinated by the fact that his right ear looks almost exactly like South America, rain forests and all. And then BAM! Suddenly you're face to face with a pop quiz

on the history of nail polish in pre-Civil War Kentucky. The worst part of it all is the sinister-looking smile on the teacher's face as she announces the pop quiz, the same sort of smile a linebacker has when he's about to blind-side a quarterback at eighty-five miles an hour. The less you're expecting a pop quiz, the more the teachers enjoy it. I had one teacher spring a quiz on me while I was in the grocery store! Fortunately, I was able to escape to the produce department, where I hid out under a pile of grapefruits until closing.

Multiple Choice Tests

You'd think these things would be easy. After all, any burphead oughta be able to get the question right when the answer is lying there right on the paper, right? Wrong! Multiple choice tests are specifically designed to mess with your head to the point that if the question was "What is your name?" you would choose (c) Mongolia. Take a look at this question from a recent biology test that was inflicted upon us:

17. The feeding habits of the Indonesian Slime Toad can best be described as:

    a)   transitory

    b)   binupial

c)   hemmenial
d)   really gross
e)   all of the above
f)   none of the above
g)   all of the above none of the time
h)   none of the above all of the time
i)   occasionally two of the above sometimes
j)   never occasionally one of the above often
k)   all of the below

Needless to say, I got a fourteen on the test.

The Word Problem

I'll take a multiple choice test any day over this next educational horror, the WORD PROBLEM. As if math tests weren't

already bad enough, somebody decided it would be fun to combine math with English, just to see if they could get an entire classroom of otherwise healthy students to lose consciousness simultaneously. It worked. Here's a word problem that was responsible for several casualties in our math class last week.

31. Lorraine is sixteen. Eleanor is seventeen and a half. If Lorraine eats seven-and-a-half pounds of Doritos while traveling east in a blue Trans Am at fifty-two mph, how many hours will she have to work out with her ThighMaster before she is

seven-eighths the age she was three days before Eleanor turned twice the age Lorraine was when she weighed one-half the weight of Don. (Hint: Don is traveling north in a green Mustang at forty-three mph and is allergic to Doritos.)

I pulled a ligament in my brain after reading this question, and several classmates experienced temporary paralysis.

I like to think that some day there will be no need for tests. In their place will be a device called the Felnerometer, which will measure how much a student has learned simply by hooking some electrodes up to his skull. Until then I continue to hope that I'll get to school one day only to find that it's been sucked into space.

The Dating Game

Maybe I caved in to peer pressure. Maybe I did it to please my parents. Most likely I did it because I had some sort of temporary brain spasm, probably caused by my accepting that dare of seeing how many paper clips I could stick up my nose during history class (forty-seven! A new school record!). Whatever the reason, I did a totally wild, irrational, and potentially dangerous thing the other day. I asked a girl out.

For me, asking a girl out was a project that required more planning than Operation Desert Storm. I spent approximately five months practicing the line, "Lynette, would you like to go out for some pizza or somethin'?" on our dog Zip, to the point that Zip now answers only to the name "Lynette." After that I created a two-foot deep trench in our living room by pacing back and forth trying to get up the nerve to actually *call* Lynette. When I finally did dial the number I did what most guys would do in this situation. I hung up as soon as someone answered the phone. This bizarre ritual continued every night for the next two months until Lynette's parents had their number changed because they thought some weirdo was calling them every night. (They were probably right.)

I had no choice but to confront Lynette face to face in school. Concentrating hard on the line I had practiced on Zip, I walked up to Lynette in the hall and said suavely, "So, Zip, would you like to go out for some pizza or something?" (Joe Cool Felner strikes again!) I about fell over when she said yes. (I found out later she thought "Zip" was some kind of new slang.)

OH, MAN! HERE COMES LYNETTE WILLIAMS! I'VE BEEN TRYING TO GET UP THE NERVE TO ASK HER OUT FOR WEEKS! NOW HERE SHE IS WALKING RIGHT BY ME!

DON'T JUST STAND THERE BONE-BRAIN! SAY HI! ASK HER OUT! TELL HER THAT HER HAIR LOOKS NICE! AT LEAST DO SOMETHING SO SHE'LL NOTICE YOU!

Life would have been a lot easier if she had just said no and if I had just taken Zip out for pizza. As it was, I spent the next three days launching into a frantic personal hygiene crusade during which I could actually *feel* nose hairs growing out of my nostrils. The more I trimmed them the faster they grew, and I was convinced that by Friday night they would evolve into giant tentacles that would lunge across the table and snatch a piece of pizza right out of Lynette's hand.

But I had an even bigger problem than my killer nose hairs or worrying that zits large enough to have their own weather systems would suddenly emerge across my face. Transportation.

In theory, I wanted to pull up to Lynette's house driving a sparkling new Corvette. In reality the only thing I've got a license to drive is my olive-green twelve-speed which has no brakes and which my mom has run over twice. What was I going to do? Tow her behind the bike in my little brother's red wagon? I had only one humiliating alternative. Dad.

Fortunately, I have a cool dad. A lot of dads would've made up some lame excuse, like they've gotta watch "Monday Night Football," even though it was Friday night. Not my dad. He seemed almost eager to drive us. I just hoped he wouldn't tell any of his knock-knock jokes or do that thing where he clears his throat and sounds like a goose with a sinus infection.

Dad and I arrived at Lynette's house at about 7:30 P.M. I would have preferred that Dad be the one to go get Lynette, seeing as how I was so nervous that I found myself forgetting to breathe. As I headed toward the door I was shaking at a rate of about two hundred spasms per second, and I must have looked like a human jackhammer bounding up their sidewalk.

I knocked on their door repeatedly, probably giving her family the impression that some kind of giant deranged woodpecker was trying to peck its way in and devour them. Her dad opened the door. Before my brain could tell my hand to stop knocking, I accidentally smacked him in the jaw and sent his dentures flying across the room and into their aquarium.

Trying to act as though my social life wasn't really turning into mush before my eyes, I managed to stammer, "Goo-goo-good-eeveming, Mr. Lynette! I'm B-B-B-uck Feller!" and stuck out my hand. I'm sure he would've shook it if he hadn't been so busy trying to rescue his teeth from a school of guppies that had begun a feeding frenzy on his dentures.

Having clearly established myself as a one hundred percent bona fide goober-head, it was time to get on with the rest of the dating process. Apparently, according to U.S. dating laws, after the guy arrives at her house, the girl is required to hide out upstairs until the next solar eclipse or until the Cleveland Browns win the Super

WHEN SHE COMES TO, I THINK I'LL ASK HER IF SHE WANTS TO SEE A MOVIE OR SOMETHING!

Bowl. In my case, I waited long enough to leave a fossilized imprint of myself in their couch. This made for plenty of torturously awkward moments talking with her parents.

Her mom began by firing a barrage of questions at me: "What-do-you-plan-to-major-in-at-college? What-about-grad-school? What-kind-of-provider-will-you-be? What-are-you-going-to-do-about-this-ozone-layer-problem?" I could actually feel my brain starting to cramp up.

Meanwhile, her dad was busy reviewing tapes of "America's Most Wanted," hitting the pause button occasionally to see if I resembled any of the police artist's sketches.

Finally, several ice ages later, Lynette appeared. At least I thought it was Lynette. It was hard to tell due to the fourteen or fifteen pounds of makeup she had cemented to her face. Eager to be debonair, I stood up only to find out that my entire left leg had been catching some serious z's and had no intention of waking up anytime soon. I looked like one of those peg-legged pirates as I hobbled over to greet her and help her to pick up several chunks of makeup that had fallen off.

After we finished gluing Lynette's makeup back on, we figured it was time to get this date on the road. We said good-bye to her parents, and Mr. Williams cheerfully reminded me that he would hunt me down and shave my head if Lynette was not home by 10:30. He also made me leave a fifty dollar deposit and took my fingerprints.

Meanwhile out in the car, my dad, having spent more time in a small confined space than most convicted felons, had tried to stave off hysterical boredom by memorizing the entire state maps of Illinois, Nebraska, and Montana. He had also managed to deplete most of the oxygen in the car and as a result was slightly delirious when I introduced him to Lynette. With a wild look in his eyes, Dad blurted out, "Lynette, what's the seventeenth largest town in Nebraska?" "Uhhh ..." "Wrong! Shermansville!" Hey, at least he didn't tell one of his knock-knock jokes.

After telling us more about Illinois, Nebraska, and Montana than most sane people want to know, Dad dropped us off at the ultimate spot for elegant cuisine: Pizza Hut. Once seated we agonized over the hundreds of critical decisions that all pizza lovers must face and wound up ordering something like "a deep-dish pizza with half mushrooms, half anchovies, two-thirds sausage, three-fifths pepperoni, one-eighth Hershey Bars, with extra super-duper wads of cheese, hold the mayo."

My main goal for the entire evening was to impress Lynette with my suaveness. So far I felt I had been fairly successful, despite smacking her dad. However, pizza and suaveness, I soon learned, do not go together. By the time our pizza arrived I was so hungry I had unconsciously downed three paper napkins and was working on a straw. As soon as the pizza hit the table I dug in as though I had just spent three months on a life raft, forgetting the fact that our pizza was approximately the same temperature as the surface of the sun. It felt like I had just swallowed a cup of lava. People told me later that my screams were heard from more than two miles away and caused dogs in several counties to begin howling. To make matters worse, a slab of molten cheese had actually fused to my chin, and it was three weeks before I could get it off.

We spent the rest of the date walking around a mall and actually had some pretty good talks, even though the molten pizza had wiped out my ability to speak anything other than the letters *l*, *g*, and *r*. Next time I think I'll play it safe and just catch a movie. (Although with my luck I'll probably get some popcorn lodged in my sinuses.)

BULKING UP

I'm definitely the victim of some major bodily deformities. I came to this conclusion about a year ago while Shirley Cosgrove and I were watching an Arnold Schwarzenegger movie (*The Regurgitator*, or something like that). I've always valued Shirley's opinion, so I asked her to rate my physique on a scale of one to ten. With her usual brutal honesty, Shirley informed me that I ranked somewhere around minus three (with Schwarzenegger being a ten and Bugs Bunny being a one). Unfortunately, she was right.

While Schwarzenegger has approximately four thousand incredibly well-developed muscles, I have five. One for each arm, one for each leg, and one that moves my head. That's it.

I've known all along that I suffer from chronic scrawniness, but I just never knew how to deal with it. For a while, I wore long-sleeved shirts to school, strategically padding my arms, legs, and shoulders with toilet paper and rolled-up newspapers. Bad decision. I ended up getting nothing but weird looks because of the strange rustling noise I made when I walked. And at a real critical moment—right when I was about to ask Lisa Bazinski out—a newspaper ad for extra-strength deodorant popped out of my collar.

It was time for something drastic. I had to do what I hated most—*work out*. But I didn't have a clue how to go about it.

HEY, KID! BEFORE YOU WORKOUT YOU GOTTA SIGN THIS FORM!

OKEY DOKEY!

MOM

WALT'S HEALTH CLUB

Fortunately for me, Shirley has become a fitness maniac and quickly volunteered to be my personal tormenter ... I mean, trainer.

We both knew that working out in the school weight room would have meant public humiliation and the destruction of my social life to the point where waving to the janitor would have been the highlight of my day. So Shirley and I sifted through the yellow pages and found *Walt's Body Building and Machoness Emporium.* (Listed under the heading "Agonizing Free-Time Activities.") Perfect.

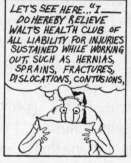

LET'S SEE HERE... "I ___ DO HEREBY RELIEVE WALT'S HEALTH CLUB OF ALL LIABILITY FOR INJURIES SUSTAINED WHILE WORKING OUT, SUCH AS HERNIAS, SPRAINS, FRACTURES, DISLOCATIONS, CONTUSIONS,

CONCUSSIONS, CONVULSIONS, SEIZURES, SPASMS, FAINTING, WHEEZING, AND HANGNAILS. PERSON TO CONTACT IN THE EVENT THAT MY HEAD GETS LODGED IN ONE OF THE WEIGHT MACHINES ___"

For $99 I was able to get a lifetime membership. Shirley suggested that improving my physique might require *two* lifetime memberships. It was great to have a trainer who had so much confidence in me.

HEY, I'LL SIGN ANYTHING IF IT'LL HELP ME GET A HEALTHIER BODY!

The first thing we noticed when we entered the weight room at Walt's was that it was filled with guys who appeared to be Neanderthals. (Though some of them may have been Cro-Magnons.) These guys had biceps the size of bowling balls, and their shoulders were developed to the point where you could no longer see their necks or half of their ears. They walked around with their arms out to the side, sort of like penguins.

They were so built-up that normal movements, such as bending over or blinking, were pretty much out of the question. On a scale of one to ten, they were fifteens, putting them somewhere between Big Foot and the Loch Ness Monster.

Believe it or not, I became a big hit with the guys at Walt's. For one thing, I had a girl for a trainer, which made me somewhat of a novelty. And for another thing, as a somewhat normal human, I could help them do things they couldn't ... like tie their shoes, scratch their backs, or open doors.

The whole experience got both Shirley and me thinking that maybe my physique wasn't so horrendous after all. Don't get me wrong. I've still been working out this past year. I just don't think I have to be built like Schwarzenegger in order to attract girls.

After a year at Walt's and Shirley's relentless workout routines, I've built myself up to a grand total of thirteen muscles, and Shirley has upgraded my physique rating to –2, which puts me somewhere around larvae. I'm sure that with another two or three years of intense workouts I'll put Bugs Bunny to shame. Most importantly, however, the days of wearing embarrassing newspaper ads to school are over.

Attack
of the Bloodmobile

When I heard that the Bloodmobile was coming to school, I knew there was no escape. Shirley, my close friend and occasional nuisance, had been on my back for months about how I should give blood regularly because the supplies were so low. I was always ready for her with a well-stocked supply of innovative excuses, such as:

1. My veins are too thin.
2. My junk food diet has created a dangerously high M&M level in my bloodstream.
3. I am allergic to the starch in nurses' uniforms.
4. The muscles in my arms are too tough to be penetrated by ordinary needles.

I didn't want Shirley to think I was completely indifferent to the blood supply problem though, so I offered to bring my dog in to donate blood. Unfortunately, my dog is an even bigger coward than I am. Deep down inside I knew the horrible truth: I was perfectly healthy, and there was absolutely no good reason that I shouldn't give blood.

Maybe I wouldn't have been so petrified of the Bloodmobile if it had a different name. Bloodmobile sounds like a vehicle from *Nightmare on Elm Street*, operated by vampires or giant alien mosquitoes. I'd feel a lot better if they called it The Sunshine Mobile or The Mr. Happy Truck and painted one of those huge smiley faces on the side. Better yet, they could disguise it as an ice cream truck, and I could fool myself into thinking I was heading off to get a shake.

One thing was certain, though. I was not alone in my fear of giving blood. Groups of students were organizing "think tanks" to come up with new, more creative excuses for not giving blood, and rumors were rampant about atrocities that occurred at last spring's blood drive: a nurse drove a needle completely through

Bryan Woodman's arm, pinning him to the table; Wayne Casman was mistakenly left on the table for two and a half hours until he had donated six gallons of blood and his blood bag looked like one of those giant red playground balls, and so on.

Despite the rumors, though, I was determined not to be a wuss this time. (I also didn't want Shirley to slap a sign on my back saying "I AM A SNIVELING WIMP!" as she had done after I avoided the bloodmobile last year.) Before my brain could convince the rest of my body to hide in my locker, I was at the gym, site of the blood drive.

If there's one thing I excel at it's shaking uncontrollably at the slightest hint of danger. Just knowing that I was in a room filled with needles and bags of blood made me look like I was experiencing my own private earthquake. As if giving blood wasn't agonizing enough, we had to wait in line to do it. This gave me plenty of time to become hysterical and start conjuring up dozens of hideous things that could go wrong, such as, they would run out of needles and resort to using straws from the cafeteria, or all the nurses would be on break when my turn came and my blood would be drawn by Dwayne the janitor.

After about an hour the moment of truth arrived, and I was strapped to a table to await my fate. I tried to distract myself by counting the various kinds of balls that were lodged in the support beams of the gym ceiling. There were three footballs, eight basketballs, two wiffleballs, two volleyballs, a soccer ball, and a BIG RED PLAYGROUND BALL LIKE WHAT WAYNE CASMAN'S BLOOD BAG TURNED INTO!!!! AAAAAAAAHHHHH!!!!! So much for distracting myself!

Out of the corner of my eye I saw the needle coming. It looked like something the Three Musketeers would have fought a duel

with, and as I recall it took four nurses to carry it. They rammed it into my arm, but I'm sure I could feel it rummaging around in my brain.

I discovered there is one advantage to having a pulse rate of 790 beats per minute. I was able to donate my pint of blood in forty-seven seconds, a new school record. Before I knew it, I was off the table and gorging myself with free pizza and brownies. It was over, and I still had all major body parts intact.

I've had a few shining moments in my life in which I was elevated to hero status. There was the time during our Little League World Series when I was hit in the head by a fastball to walk in the winning run. And another time when I helped to rescue a drowning chipmunk during a church picnic.

But neither of these moments could compare to the feeling I had after giving blood. It was incredible! I, Buck Felner, the kid who is consistently picked last in gym class, had saved somebody's life. Along with the other kids in the gym that day we saved 272 lives, the equivalent of the starting line-ups of the National League and The American League combined! Best of all, it happened without a single person being pinned to a table by Dwayne the janitor using straws from the cafeteria.

So if you're feeling kind of wimpy and you'd like to convert yourself into an instant hero, I have two words for you. GIVE BLOOD! You won't feel a thing, except the free brownies and pizza sliding down your throat.

Home Alone

I've got to say, I was pretty psyched up about this weekend. At last, my first chance to have the house to myself. The opportunities seemed nearly endless: staying up until 4:00 A.M. to watch mindless movies on the Ultra Late, Late, Late Show, making pizza milkshakes, testing the effects of the microwave on various objects, such as my little brother's Ninja Turtle action figures, some stick deodorant, and my math book. Yeah, it was going to be a great weekend.

Mom, Dad, and my little brother, Louis, left at about 5:00 P.M. Friday, headed for the Toledo Museum of Opera. Personally, I would rather spend a week locked in my Algebra class than spend an hour at the Toledo Museum of Opera. I definitely lucked out. I was on my own and ready to start my bachelor weekend.

It began with a wholesome home-cooked meal: hot dogs coated in Hershey sauce. Excellent. Then I cranked up the stereo. I had it up so loud I couldn't understand the words. In fact, I couldn't even tell what kind of music it was. It didn't matter. Loudness was the key. Sitting in our living room that Friday night was like sticking your head inside a jet engine right before take-off. I loved it. At one point I got too close to one of the speakers and the force blew all the hair off my arm. It still hasn't grown back.

Yep, things were going great for old bachelor Buck. The stereo was cranked, I was watching *The Terminator* on HBO and trying to read Schwarzenegger's lips (which is pretty impossible since I can't understand him even when I can hear what he's saying), and the blender was on high, whipping up a delicious pizza shake. Ahh, what a life! Unfortunately, this ecstasy was short-lived. All of a sudden, there was a popping noise, then a fizzing sound, a

loud clank, and things went black. There was silence.

It took me a while to realize I had blown a fuse. In fact, as I later discovered, I had blown our entire electrical box. It melted. There I was, in the dark at 11:30 P.M., with no electricity, and a whole weekend ahead of me. Suddenly, the Toledo Museum of Opera seemed like a great place to be.

The thing to do, of course, was to find a flashlight. But, in order to find a flashlight I needed a flashlight, and the flashlight was in the basement. Now I'm not normally a wimp when it comes to the dark. Sure, I had to sleep with the light on until I was eleven, and in recent years I used to lie in bed in the dark and imagine that my dresser was actually a crazed gym teacher who had come to make me do fourteen thousand push-ups. But I've gotten over all of that. Our basement, however, was the last place that I wanted to be at midnight, alone, with no lights.

Going into our basement that night was like walking into a Stephen King novel. Suddenly, every horror movie I had ever seen was flashing through my brain. I went down the stairs at a speed of about one step every seventeen minutes. With each one I expected to step on a tentacle or a giant drooling, killer-lizard,

or a skull. By 3:00 A.M. I had made it to the bottom. I felt my way along the wall to the other side with my heart pounding loud enough to wake up the neighbors. Miraculously, I found the flashlight. I turned it on. There was a delayed reaction, and then the light came on, with a beam about as powerful as the light given off by an elderly firefly.

I shined the beam around the basement. I could sort of make things out. The furnace, some old bikes, what appeared to be a pile of old tires. And then, I saw something that made my hair stand on end. There, standing ten feet in front of me, slobbering in the dark, stood the most hideous creature I had ever seen. Six feet tall with huge veins spewing out of its head, looking for a meal. There wasn't a second to spare. I searched for a weapon, and by sheer luck my hand latched on to something solid. It was my brother's Big Wheel tricycle. I lunged at the creature, screaming "Ahhhhhhh!!!!" and swinging the trike crazily. It put up a strong fight, but I had obviously caught it off-guard, and I beat it relentlessly until it groaned and fell over, warm liquid gushing out of it.

I stayed there shaking in the basement until morning. As the sunlight began to stream into the basement I slowly began to realize that the monster I had defended our home against was the hot water tank. Death by tricycle. It was totally mangled. My brother's Big Wheel wasn't much better off. It looked like someone had taken it for a test drive in a mine field.

Between the melted fuse box, the hot water tank, and the Big Wheel, my bachelor weekend cost me $1,100. I'm also grounded until I'm thirty-five. But I learned an important lesson: *Always* keep the volume on the stereo below eight when you're watching TV and making a pizza shake. Otherwise you could blow something.

Broadway Buck

Extracurricular activities have never been one of my strengths. (I have trouble just saying the word *extracurricular*!) Until recently, my after-school activities consisted of two little-known clubs. I did a six-week stint in the Future Taxidermists of America (FTA) but quit when I found out all the animals we'd be stuffing were road kills. Then I joined the Weeding Club. Their sole objective is to weed neglected areas in the community, such as the alley behind Burger King, miscellaneous sidewalks, and the entire football field. (The only reason I joined was there were just two other members and I could instantly become vice president in charge of crabgrass.)

But when somebody suggested I join the Drama Club, I figured *why not?* Anything would be better than the Weeding Club, and this might very well lead to a highly successful movie career.

So I found myself sitting in the auditorium on a rainy Wednesday afternoon with eighty other kids, all of whom were murmuring to each other that Drama Club might very well lead *them* to highly successful movie careers.

The first order of business was to choose the school play for the year. Wayne Scrogner suggested *Jurassic Park*. That drew enthusiastic responses from everyone until we realized we'd be fighting over who would get to play the T. Rex.

Lorraine Uttleman suggested *The Hunt for Red October*. She felt the metal shop classes could easily build the necessary submarines. I blurted out *Dances with Wolves*, recommending

that the entire freshman class could be stampeded across the stage wearing woolly, brown suits for the buffalo scenes. Tons of other exciting possibilities were tossed around, such as *Jaws*, *Star Wars*, and *Speed*.

We were getting increasingly fired up about each one until Mrs. Clegman, our Drama Club adviser, stood up and said, *"Oklahoma!"* None of us were too keen on doing *Oklahoma*. But Mrs. Clegman diplomatically screeched, "Oklahoma!! We *will* be performing Oklahoma!!!" at decibel levels that could knock the hair off a yak from fifty yards. So we all agreed that *Oklahoma* would be a most excellent play for us to perform, especially since we had no choice.

The next step in our show business careers was tryouts. The tryout process is a very simple one whereby you, the tryoutee, stand on stage and sing the song of your choice. Meanwhile, fellow Drama Club members (and hoards of other people who have stopped by to watch you make a complete nimrod of yourself) try to suppress hysterical laughter. I, for one, showed a real talent for behaving like a total dufus in front of a large audience. When the accompanist asked what I'd be singing, all I could think of was the theme from "Magnum P.I." This would have been a pretty cool selection if it had had words.

I hummed along for a while and then started making up words as I went. "Whoa, Magnum P.I. Yeah! Tom Selleck, cruisin' around in a hot red car! Oh, yeah! Got his Detroit Tigers cap on! Whoa, yeah! Higgins hangin' out with his dogs, yeah, whoa!"

Needless to say, throngs of screaming girls did not rush the stage demanding dates with me. Throngs of girls did, however, run screaming for the exits. I was told later that passersby mistook my singing for the sound of someone torturing a rat with a hot poker.

Miraculously, however, I was offered a part in *Oklahoma*. Maybe it was because only four guys tried out compared to sixty-five girls. In fact, I was given *seven* parts in the play. My roles included Third Cowpoke, Cattle Rustler with Bad Hiccups, and Guy on a Fence with Sore Foot.

Memorizing my lines was difficult for me since I have trouble remembering my locker number. I found it helpful to write my lines on the back of another actor's neck (usually while she was sleeping in home room).

To make my situation even tougher, some of my characters actually spoke to each other. I'd say, "Boy-howdy! Do I ever have some fearsome hiccups!" Then I'd have to scramble across the stage, change shirts behind a fake cow, and reply to myself, "Hiccups! You wouldn't give a hoot about any old hiccups if your foot was as sore as mine!"

Most of the audience thought I was either hallucinating or playing a character with multiple personalities.

All in all I had a blast doing *Oklahoma,* except for the time when I danced off the stage into the orchestra pit and got my foot stuck in a tuba. I'm already looking forward to next year's rendition of *Back to the Future, Parts I, II* and *III.*

COUNTDOWN TO SUMMER

At this moment there are exactly seven days, six hours, thirty-seven minutes, and twenty-two seconds of school left. I'm severely psyched. No more waiting around in sub-zero temperatures and seventy-mile-an-hour winds only to find out that I missed the bus for the eighty-seventh consecutive day. No more eating cafeteria food that looks like something my dog threw up. No more dealing with seniors who weigh 250 pounds—and whose idea of a good time is seeing how many underclassmen will fit into a standard-sized gym locker (seven is the current record).

Yep, the carefree days of lounging around, soaking up harmful ultra-violet rays, and swatting kindergartner-sized mosquitoes are just around the corner. Unfortunately, there are still some critical steps that have to be taken before another grueling school year is laid to rest.

Step 1:
Locker Cleanout

I've been thinking about patenting an invention that would save us all a lot of time, hassle, and nausea: disposable lockers.

About the last thing I want to do is start pawing through nine months worth of rotting locker entrails, most of which are no longer recognizable. I'd rather just

pick up the phone and call in a hazardous-waste disposal team. They could haul the stuff off and bury it … in a lead container … several miles below the floor of the Indian Ocean. During the summer, the janitors could simply go through and install fresh lockers.

It's been about two months since I've even gone near my locker. And it's not just because there's no room in it. My locker partner and I agreed: One whiff of the thing could cripple a bull elephant.

Last year it took me three days and four dumpsters to clean out my locker. Here is some of what I found inside:

1. Gym clothes that had fused tight against the inside of the locker to the point that I needed an acetylene torch to get them out.
2. A trombone (at least, it used to be a trombone).
3. Forty-three sneakers, most of which did not match.
4. Textbooks I had completely forgotten about.
5. Three half-eaten medium pizzas with sausage.
6. The transmission of an '83 Buick Regal (don't even ask).
7. Fourteen Glade air fresheners.

8. A waffle iron.
9. Thirty-seven various life forms.

You can see why the hazardous-waste disposal team would come in handy.

Step 2: Signing Yearbooks

At our school, getting your yearbook signed has become a serious fad, with the main objective to get as many signatures as possible. Not all signatures, however, carry the same weight. Here's how it boils down:

Signer	Points
Regular Joe-Blow student	1
Upperclassman	2
Member of football team	3
Any cheerleader	5
Homecoming queen	10
Vice principal	−1

The result of all this is that you wind up combing the school for anybody who looks remotely familiar, yelling things like: "Hey! You! I saw you in the library once! Sign my yearbook!"

When somebody does sign your yearbook, he signs it as though you're about to leave on a twelve-year exploration of Saturn, using patented phrases like "Don't ever change!" or "I'll never forget you, man." Most of these are from people who probably live next door to you, and whom you'll see all summer long.

Step 3: Report Cards

The way I see it, report cards are one last way for the school administration to torment us before our big summer escape.

They know they can no longer assign essay questions that ask us to discuss (in 1,000 words or less) the invention of mustard and its effect on Third World soccer goalies.

They can't ask us what the cube root of 1,784 is when they notice that we've completely zoned out during algebra, and they can't ask us to climb the ropes in gym class using only our right hands.

So they take one last jab at us by giving out report cards on pieces of paper about the size of billboards. Then they pass them out so slowly that we'll agonize over whether we used a number 2 pencil to fill in the computerized final exam answer sheets (knowing that a number 3 pencil will doom us to a lifetime of working at a gas station).

But once you've sandblasted your locker, signed two hundred yearbooks, received your report card, and regained consciousness, you're free. Proceed directly to summer.

Working for a Living

Well, the school year has finally gasped its last breath, and we have leaped into summer vacation full force. This is not always good news. For many of us, summer vacation means days of intense boredom, highlighted by such mind-expanding endeavors as seeing how many flies we can stuff into our sister's purse before she goes out on her big date and trying to find some way to get the dog to mow the lawn.

To combat these potentially toxic levels of boredom among teenagers, scientists developed summer jobs. Yeah, I know, most of you would rather sing along with your little brother while he watches seven straight hours of "Barney" episodes than take a summer job. But when you realize that if you stay home you'll have to clean the garage, paint the house, and reseal the driveway virtually every day, a summer job starts to look like a pretty decent escape.

There are some definite do's and don'ts when it comes to landing that ideal summer job and the hefty minimum wage paycheck that comes with it. Let's review some of the do's.

Do:

1. Fill out the application neatly.
2. Arrive for your interview on time.
3. Wear a suit and tie to the interview.
4. Have good posture and smile often.
5. Speak clearly and confidently.
6. Cover up that tattoo on your arm that says "INSANITY RULES!"

But even more important than what you should do when trying to get a job is what you *shouldn't* do.

Don't:

1. Fill out the application in crayon or finger paints.
2. Arrive for your interview wearing only cut-off shorts and no shirt.
3. Ask the interviewer to refer to you by your nickname (i.e., "Hurler" or "Scab Man").
4. Wipe your nose on your sleeve.
5. Wipe your nose on the interviewer's sleeve.
6. Nervously reach across the desk and fidget with the interviewer's tie, occasionally stapling it to papers on his desk.
7. Ask the interviewer if anyone has ever told him or her that he or she looks like Granny from "The Beverly Hillbillies."

By following these tips closely you should be able to get a job no later than mid-August, which, after taxes, will give you enough money to buy such extravagant items as a comb, or maybe a sock.

I know what many of you are going to say now. You're going to say, "But, Buck, I've had summer jobs before. They were so dull that por-tions of my brain have become perma-nently numb, and I have trouble distin-guishing shades of green. What can I do

on this summer's job to keep from becoming so bored that I gnaw all of the hair off my arms?" I'm glad you asked that. The answer is you have to look for creative ways to liven up your job. Take a look at this example:

Let's say you've just landed a job as third assistant vice-stockboy in charge of pickles at Ultra Food Genie Grocery World. On the surface this job appears to be about as stimulating as getting a job as a human road cone. But with a little creativity you'll love the job so much you'll work double shifts and will start sleeping in the cabbage display area rather than waste precious time driving to and from work. Here are just a few ways to put some zing into this job.

Step 1: Wear Rollerblades on the Job.

You'll have to clear this with your manager, but once he sees how much more quickly you can stock shelves on skates, he'll have to agree to it. Grocery store floors are excellent for rollerblading and you'll have a blast cruising down crowded aisles trying to avoid hitting customers. You can even make a game out of it, scoring points as follows: bumping a customer, –10; knocking a customer over, –25; giving a customer a concussion, –50; with 0 being a perfect score.

Step 2: Eat All the Food You Want for Free.

Since many grocery foods have expiration dates and the

store often is unable to sell all of the food before it expires, ask if you can eat it. This can mean truckloads of donuts, cookies, ice cream, pies, etc. Granted, many of these items will be covered with green fuzzy stuff, but eating them shouldn't cause any harmful side effects, other than occasional convulsions.

Step 3: Paint Faces on the Melons.

This can be an excellent way to hone your artistic skills, while simultaneously adding some flair to the Produce Department. You may want to choose a theme for your melon faces, such as U.S. Presidents, the cast of "Beverly Hills 90210," or people who have turned you down for dates.

Step 4: Rewire the checkout scanners.

Rewire the checkout scanners so that instead of giving off the normal "beep" sound with each item, they emit the sound of barking dobermans. If you're at all handy with electronics, this is easy to do and very entertaining.

I hope you've found my guide to summer employment informative. If you follow it carefully you should be able to leave your job at the end of the summer with all the hair on your arms intact and without any numbness in your brain. Good luck!

BUCK ON FRIENDS

You can never have too many friends—at least that's what they say. And I tend to agree, except when it's your turn to treat for pizza. People seem to use the term "friend" in a lot of different ways. For some people, all you've got to do to be their friend is to have sat next to them on the bus one time. To be considered a friend of other people you have to have done something really intense, like drag them from a burning building or warn them that there's something hanging out of their nose. Anyway, it's pretty clear that there are a lot of different kinds of friends, and I thought maybe I should take some time to talk about some of the basic types of friends that I've encountered.

The Whiner Friend

This is the friend who is constantly complaining to you about everything, from not having enough "fizz" in the soda that he's drinking to worrying that his eyebrows are going bald. People like this have been whining so long that their voices have begun to sound like the noise a mosquito makes when it's caught in your ear.

I've got this friend, Marty. Great guy, except for the fact that he's caught in a state of perpetual whininess. I know. I stayed overnight at his house one time, and he whined in his sleep. (His *dog* even whines!) Every once in a while, when Marty's *really* bummed out about something (like maybe his shoe came untied or he swallowed his gum), he kicks into what I call "turbo-whine," which is about fourteen thousand deci-

bels louder than his normal whine. If I'm within one hundred feet of Marty when he's in turbo-whine mode, the noise sets up a kind of harmonic frequency that actually makes my brain vibrate and my vision blurry. I'm confident that if Marty won forty million dollars in the Publisher's Clearing House Sweepstakes, he'd complain that he pulled a muscle in his back from carrying his money home.

The Shy Friend

This kind of friend can be real frustrating. When the two of you do stuff together, he's a wild man. He'll use his Super Soaker water cannon to feed chocolate syrup to his dog. He'll gargle your little brother's goldfish. He'll do this trick where he blows air out of the corner of his left eye. But when you get him around your other friends, who you've been raving to about him for weeks, he suddenly develops the personality of a boll weevil. He'll go so far as to act grossed out when one of your other friends eats a piece of spaghetti and gets it to come out his nose.

The Do-You-One-Better Friend

You know who I'm talkin' about here. You get done telling an incredible true story about the time Kirby Puckett's car broke down in front of your house and he stayed overnight and taught you how to hit a fastball and autographed your little brother's head, and your friend will scoff and tell about the time the LA Raiders' bus broke down in front of *his* house and they *all* stayed overnight and liked it so much they decided to make his house their summer training camp and signed him up to start at cornerback for their '93 season. It's easy to tell when you're dealing with a do-you-one-better friend, because every sentence they ever speak begins with "That's nothing! One time I ..."

The Best Friend

Hopefully, all of you have got one of these. You'll know if you do because this person will come through in the clutch when the other friends leave you hangin'. He's the guy who, if he's captain of a basketball team in gym class, will pick you first even though he knows his four-year-old sister could out-play you blindfolded and wearing hip boots. And when your little brother decides one night that it might be fun to hack off most of your hair with the weed eater while you're sleeping, your best friend will convince you that it looks excellent and you'll probably start a hot new trend, even though everyone in school thinks you look like the lead in *Alien III*.

In short, your best friend is the one who can put up with you in spite of your occasional dorkwad behavior. He doesn't care if you whine about stupid stuff. He doesn't care if you're always trying to top his stories. And he still likes you even if his other friends think you're about as much fun as a sinus infection. Treat him well. People like him are hard to find.

Wheezin'
Down the Highway

When our youth pastor announced that our upcoming outing was going to be a forty-mile overnight bike trip to Lake Slag, there were shrieks of approval. Not that we were all that psyched about a bike trip. (For some of us our past biking experience consisted of doing several hundred thousand laps around our driveway when we were ten.) But a bike trip had to be at least five thousand times less boring than our three previous outings: a field trip to the Ohio Museum of Mortuary Science, a scavenger hunt and overnight at the County Environmental Waste Processing Center (alias, landfill), and a day tour of a nearby kitty litter factory.

Preparing for our trip would not be easy. It would require precision planning (i.e., deciding which of my shirts best highlights my rippling forearms, thereby impressing girls on the trip), intensive training (I would jog to the TV set whenever I changed the channel), and, most important, rescuing my bike from the impenetrable wasteland which we referred to as our garage.

The last time a car was parked in our garage was during the Carter Administration. Then, one day, somebody left a skateboard in the middle of the floor, and other objects steadily began to gravitate towards the garage, until most of the things we owned were in the garage. Now it looked like the aftermath of the World Trade Center bombing. It took three days of hacking through the rubble with the help of a blowtorch, a back hoe, and the Jaws of Life from our local rescue squad, but I did at last locate the fossilized remains of my bike.

I worked on my bike for two solid days bending, reshaping, hammering, and polishing, until it reached a point that four out of ten people, when asked, "What is this?" would reply, "Well, it sort of looks like a bike ... or else a tuba. Yeah, that's it! It's a tuba!" I tossed the bike into a dumpster and borrowed my neighbor's bike.

At long last the big day had arrived. We converged on our church at eight o'clock on a Saturday morning, and I quickly began to realize that compared to the rest of the group I was pretty poorly prepared. The first thing that stood out was my helmet. I didn't have a bike helmet, so I was wearing an old San Francisco 49ers helmet that I found (where else) in our garage. This prompted a barrage of wisecracks such as, "Wow! I didn't know Joe Montana was coming on the trip!" to which I fired back, "Montana plays for the Chiefs now, wombat!"

Next I started to feel self-conscious about my bike, mostly due to Eric Gratzman droning on about how his bike was made out of cold-extruded chrome-moly 301 alloy, weighed less than a volleyball, and had twenty-eight speeds. "What's yours made out of?" he asked. "Ummm, metal," I replied, trying nonchalantly to cover up the large K-Mart emblem.

About the only thing I had that was remotely trendy was a pair of biking shorts I had gotten for Christmas. Wearing these things is about as comfortable as wearing a pair of underwear that fit you when you were in second grade. They were so tight that my legs slowly began turning blue, and I had lost all feeling from the knee down in both legs. I tried to be optimistic, though. The blue of my legs went well with my black shorts, and if I fell and scraped my legs I probably wouldn't feel a thing.

At 8:45, we finally hit the road. I knew I was in trouble when I found myself out of breath just from climbing onto the bike. Ten minutes into the trip I was seriously hurtin'. I was breathing so hard that my nostrils made a loud flapping sound when I exhaled and sweating so badly that there was a constant puddle under my bike. It didn't surprise anyone to see vultures doing slow circles above my head.

Things quickly got worse. When I looked up and saw a hill the size of Mount McKinley that we had to go up, I fainted several times, only to be awakened each time by hitting my head  on the handlebars. *Cars* were having trouble going up this hill, and I kept expecting to see an expedition of hikers trying to scale the thing. I was going so slow that people driving by couldn't even see my legs moving. It didn't help my spirits any to see a caterpillar breeze by me on the right.

97

After what seemed to be enough time in which to complete a college education, we finally reached the top and rested. Our hearts were pounding so intensely that our bodies swelled to twice their normal sizes with each beat. Now it was time to cruise down the hill.

Normally I would look forward to flying down a hill on a bike. But going down this hill was like riding down Mount Everest. In a matter of seconds I was going so fast that the force of the wind stretched the corners of my mouth back behind my ears and my lower lip started slapping against my chest. My eyes were watering so badly that Shirley Cosgrove, who was riding behind me, thought it was raining. When I started to pass cars and trucks I knew I was hitting speeds that no Felner had hit before.

I was actually starting to enjoy it all, though, when I saw the dog. An evil, snarling, crazed, lightning-fast dog. Suddenly I felt like an antelope on one of those nature shows. I kept hoping the predator would set his sights on someone else in the herd, but he clearly decided he wanted to dine on some fileted Felner. He made one pass and chomped into my ankle (fortunately I didn't feel it because my leg was numb from my tight shorts). I quickly grabbed my water bottle and gave him a squirt up one nostril. He let go and regrouped. He made another pass, grabbed my left sneaker, and swallowed it whole. He launched several more attacks during which he snatched a rear reflector, my watch, the tire pump, three spokes, and my shirt. Then he circled around in front of me for the kill.

It was a major goof-up on his part. Hitting him was unavoidable. I nailed him broadside, and suddenly I was airborne. I felt like one of those kids riding their bikes into space at the end of *E.T.* I passed some robins, terrified a woman who was sitting on a second story balcony, and landed in a swimming pool.

When I came to I was floating in an inner tube. My neighbor's bike was on the roof of a house and was so mangled that it looked like, well, a tuba.

Needless to say, I didn't make it to Lake Slag that day. Our youth pastor arranged a ride home for me, and I spent the rest of the day watching nature shows, trying to pull the corners of my mouth back from behind my ears, and cutting my biking shorts off with a pair of scissors. Meanwhile, I'm trying to work up the courage to tell my neighbor about his bike. My hope is that he's had a lifelong desire to own a tuba.

There's No Place Like Home

Now don't get me wrong. I *love* home. After all, home is where the heart is, as well as the stereo, the refrigerator, my mountain bike, and other items essential to sustaining life. But by late July I was ready to join the French Foreign Legion just to get a break from home.

Part of the problem was my Dad. Dad's got the incredible ability of being able to *see* grass grow. When most people look and see a beautifully manicured lawn, Dad sees grass growing uncontrollably. As a result, I've been mowing our three-quarter acre lawn approximately once every three hours. When I wasn't mowing the lawn (which was basically at night and during severe hail storms), Mom kept me busy with projects, such as sealing the driveway, cleaning up our toxic waste site (otherwise known as the basement), and scraping the tar off the kitchen floor, tracked in by people who had walked on the recently sealed driveway.

I needed a change. I needed to be out on my own. I needed to get away before I acted on my overwhelming urge to hurl the lawn mower in front of a high-speed train. I needed summer camp.

Although I had never gone to summer camp, I envisioned what it would be like: sleeping until nine or ten, floating around a beautiful mountain lake on an air mattress, dining on excellent camp food. Yep, two weeks at Camp Itchy-Hemp was just the ticket, I thought.

I was seriously misinformed.

In late July, I eagerly climbed on the Camp Itchy-Hemp bus. Normally, I would have noticed the fact that the other campers, those who had survived previous sentences at Camp Itchy-Hemp, were either sobbing uncontrollably or trying desperately to use the zippers on their jackets to saw through the bars on the bus windows. But I was too thrilled to be out of the house without a lawn mower attached to my hands to notice much of anything.

When we arrived at Camp Itchy-Hemp the first order of business was being assigned bunks.

Given a choice, most people would choose sleeping on a library shelf over sleeping on a bunk bed at Itchy-Hemp. There were approximately ten inches between the top of one bunk and the bottom of another. Some kids had to be stuffed into their bunks by counselors using crowbars. Once in your bunk, you couldn't inhale more than one cubic inch of air with each breath for fear of cracking a rib. The mattresses, if there were any, provided about as much padding as the *New York Times* sports section.

Of course, they didn't give us the luxury of lounging around in these fine accommodations for long. At 5:30 A.M. the guards, I mean, counselors, would burst into the bunkhouse and herd us all down to the shore for a mind-numbing swim in the thirty-three degree waters of Lake Grackle. This is the kind of water where sticking your foot into it causes you to inhale nonstop for about the next week and a half. Submerging your whole body in it (as we idiots did) causes your heart rate to slow down to about one beat every four days and results in permanent hair loss.

After a hearty breakfast of what looked and tasted like paper mache (we found out later it *was* paper mache), it was time for chores. Chores ran pretty much straight through from 6:30 A.M. to 10 P.M., with time out to tend to poisonous snake bites and to capture other campers who were trying to paddle their way to freedom on the diving raft. Yep, the staff at Itchy-Hemp had a special talent for creating chores. Waxing the flagpole, raking the woods, dusting the basketball court. You name it, we did it, including the mother of all camp chores, latrine duty.

Our reward for having performed fifteen hours of nonstop prison-gang type labor was that we got to crawl back to our bunk

houses and wedge ourselves into our crummy little bunks (although many of us had to be dragged back to bed by the counselors).

I returned home looking like a giant, walking blister, but I had a totally new outlook. Mow the lawn? Seal the driveway? No problem! Not when you've got three great home-cooked meals a day and an actual bed. My camping days are history.

Water, Water Everywhere

It was a typical July afternoon. Sitting outside, even in the shade, was about as refreshing as wallowing in a lava flow, and it had been so humid over the last couple of weeks that moss had started to grow on my legs. To top things off, six weeks of summer vacation had left me so bored that I was actually looking for chores to do. (At one point, in a bout of boredom, I washed and waxed our wheelbarrow.) I was, therefore, extremely fired up when Shirley called up and said seven words that would permanently alter my life: "Wild and Wicked Water World is open!"

Water parks, for those of you who have spent the last five years in a cave, are a relatively new phenomenon whereby you pay ten bucks to slide down what are basically just souped-up sewer pipes. It may not sound like much, but to me it was a way to avoid having to spend the next five hours polishing the weedeater. I was out the door before I had my shoes on.

I had a hint that maybe this wasn't going to be a carefree summer afternoon when I read the sign at the entrance to the park.

WARNING: ENTER AT YOUR OWN RISK! WILD AND WICKED WATER WORLD IS NOT RESPONSIBLE FOR LOSS OF TEETH, LIMBS, OR MAJOR ORGANS. PEOPLE WITH THE FOLLOWING CONDITIONS WOULD BE OUT OF THEIR MINDS TO COME IN HERE:

HIGH BLOOD PRESSURE
BACK TROUBLE
FEAR OF HEIGHTS
FEAR OF WATER
DANDRUFF
COMMON SENSE

Suddenly, polishing the weedeater seemed pretty tempting. But I didn't want to look like a wimp in front of Shirley, so I controlled the overwhelming urge to run screaming towards the exit.

Except for the rides themselves, everything at the park was paved. Getting from one ride to the next on a sunny day was like running across a giant, hot skillet. The result was huge mobs of people twitching their way across the pavement like a bunch of spastic chickens, simultaneously shrieking "Oooooh! Oh! Aaaaah! Ooooh!"

Shirley and I screamed our way across a huge stretch of molten pavement and hobbled towards the Twin Turbo Tubes of Terror. The Twin Tubes start at the top of a six-story tower and are braided together so that not only are you hurtling down at speeds that an Indy 500 driver would be proud of, you are also twirling around. They are basically a straight drop for five-and-a-half stories until they curve and spit their victims into a big pool, where a crew from the show "Rescue 911" is waiting, hoping to film their next episode. Judging by the mob of people waiting in line, you would have thought that we were all waiting to have a private dinner with the President. If things moved quickly I figured we'd get to the top of the tubes sometime

around noon on Friday. I didn't complain, though. It gave me time to work on an excuse.

Unfortunately, the sight of the tube tower, which at times disappeared into the clouds, caused most of the blood to drain from my brain, and therefore the closest I came to making up an excuse was to mumble "Uhhhh" for about twenty minutes straight.

Funny how time flies when you're petrified. Before I knew it we were at the top. I could actually feel my pulse beating in my hair as I climbed zombielike into one of the tubes and waited for one of the lifeguards to signal that the tube was clear for me to go ahead and mangle myself. Shirley climbed into the other tube, and we were off.

The first thing I noticed was my eyelids. They began to flap noisily in the wind as I picked up more and more speed. Water was going so far up into my nose that it started to seep into my brain, and my nostrils flared to five times their normal size, making a loud whistling noise the whole time. I figured I was going somewhere between 180 and 220 miles an hour while simultaneously spiraling around in a circle. It felt like I had been flushed down some kind of huge, evil toilet. Fortunately, I fainted about halfway down and was spared the rest of the experience. The next thing I remember

I was flying out of the bottom of the tube. I skimmed across the water and finally came to rest on top of a bald guy who, delirious from his ride, thought that he was the victim of an airline crash at sea.

That was a week ago. My nostrils still haven't returned to their normal size, and most of the hair on my head was blown off, including my eyebrows. I'm also missing a large mole that had been on my left arm. But the whole experience has given me a new appreciation for working around the house. Now I'm actually looking forward to steam-cleaning the furnace.